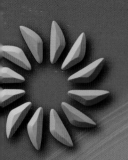

DISCOVER RAYS

by Susan H. Gray

Cherry Lake Publishing • Ann Arbor, Michigan

3

CHERRY LAKE
Publishing

Published in the United States of America
by Cherry Lake Publishing
Ann Arbor, Michigan
www.cherrylakepublishing.com

Content Adviser: Dominique A. Didier, PhD, Associate Professor, Department of
Biology, Millersville University
Reading Adviser: Marla Conn, ReadAbility, Inc

Photo Credits: © aslysun/Shutterstock Images, cover; © Tatiana Belova/
Shutterstock Images, 4; © dive-hive/Shutterstock Images, 6; © Santhosh
Varghese/Shutterstock Images, 8; © Kjersti Joergensen/Shutterstock Images, 10;
© A Cotton Photo/Shutterstock Images, 12; © Jung Hsuan/Shutterstock
Images, 14; © renacal1/iStock, 16; © frantisekhojdysz/Shutterstock Images, 18;
Ariel Bravy/Shutterstock Images, 20

Library of Congress Cataloging-in-Publication Data
Gray, Susan Heinrichs, author.
 [Rays]
 Discover rays / Susan H. Gray.
    pages cm.—(Splash!)
 Summary: "This Level 3 guided reader introduces basic facts about rays,
including their physical characteristics, diet, and habitat. Simple callouts ask the
student to think in new ways, supporting inquiry-based reading. Additional text
features and search tools, including a glossary and an index, help students
locate information and learn new words."—Provided by publisher.
 Audience: Ages 6–10
 Audience: K to grade 3
 Includes bibliographical references and index.
 ISBN 978-1-63362-604-1 (hardcover)—ISBN 978-1-63362-694-2 (pbk.)—
ISBN 978-1-63362-784-0 (pdf)—ISBN 978-1-63362-874-8 (ebook)
 1. Rays (Fishes)—Juvenile literature. I. Title.

QL638.8.G73 2016
597.3'5—dc23
                                            2015005515

Cherry Lake Publishing would like to acknowledge the work of the Partnership
for 21st Century Skills. Please visit www.p21.org for more information.

Printed in the United States of America
Corporate Graphics

TABLE OF CONTENTS

4

Flat Swimmer

What kind of animal is this creature? It lives in the sea. It swims. It has wide fins. Its body is flat. And it has a tail. This animal is a ray. It is a kind of fish.

Rays' fins help them swim.

Most rays live in the ocean. They live in warm water. The water can be shallow or deep. They swim quietly through the water.

This ray's flat body helps it glide through the ocean.

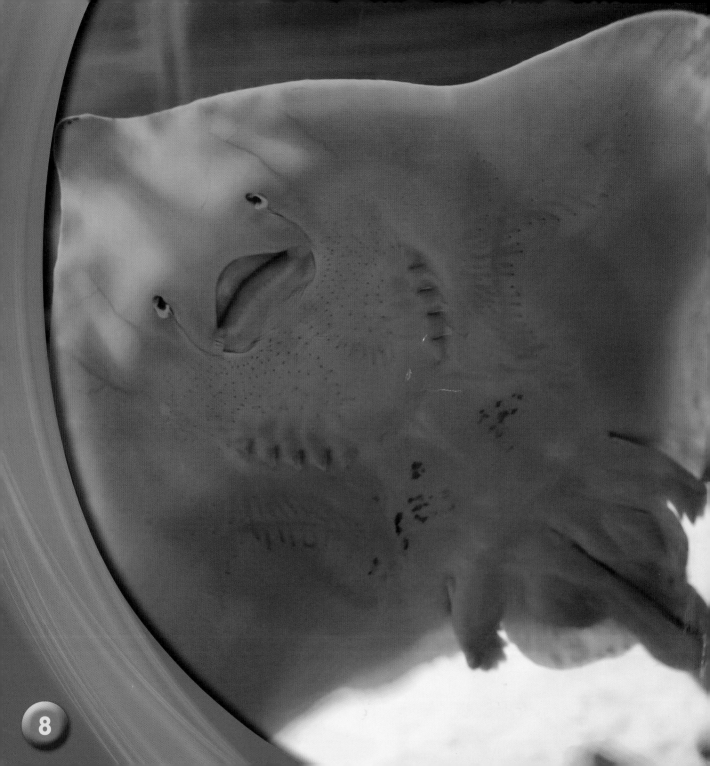

8

The main part of the ray's body is the **disk**. Some rays have a round disk. Some have a diamond-shaped disk. Eyes are on top of the disk. The mouth is underneath.

THINK!

An electric ray has two lumps behind its head. These lumps can produce an electrical **shock**. Why would a ray need to shock something?

This ray looks like it has a face, but that is only its mouth and nostrils.

The Day of a Ray

What do rays do all day? They swim, rest, and eat. Some glide around with their big mouths open. **Plankton** get scooped up into their mouths. This is how some rays eat.

This ray is catching plankton in its open mouth.

11

Other rays use their **snouts** to find food. They poke around in the sand. There, they dig up crabs and worms to eat.

This ray is searching for food on the ocean floor.

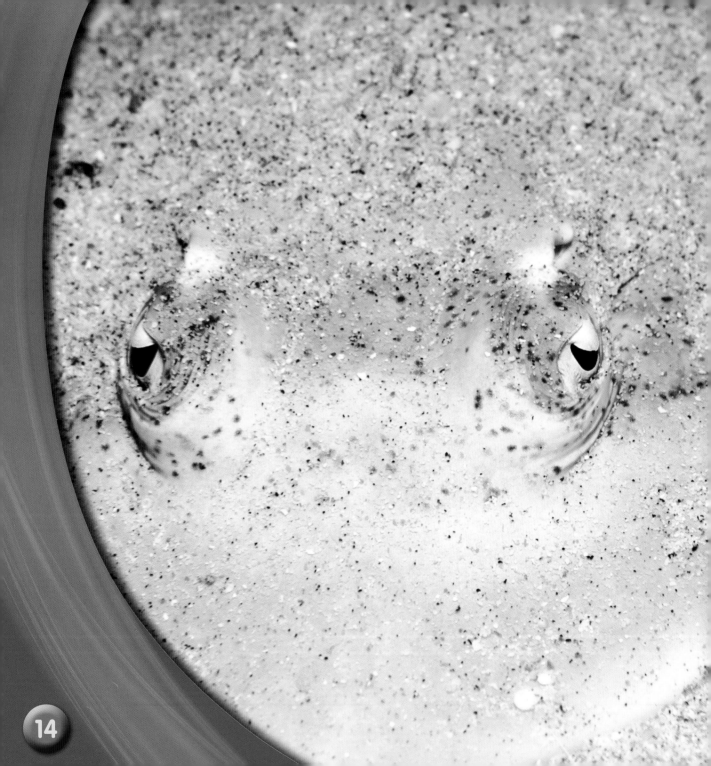

Some rays use **camouflage**. They lie very still on the seafloor, watching for **prey**. Soon a fish comes by. It does not notice the ray. The ray quickly grabs the fish and swallows it.

MAKE A GUESS!

What do you think would happen if this ray's skin had bright colors and patterns?

This ray has buried itself in the sand.

Rays are good swimmers. They move smoothly through the water. Sometimes, they leap into the air. They might even turn a flip. Then they splash back into the sea. No one knows why. Maybe they are just playing.

Rays sometimes leap out of the water.

All Kinds of Rays

Rays come in many colors and sizes. They can be blue, brown, or gray. Some are covered with little white dots. Others have blue spots.

In some places, scuba divers can get close enough to take photos of rays.

The biggest ray could cover your bedroom floor. The smallest ray would fit on a **saucer**. Plain or spotted, large or small—rays are amazing animals.

ASK QUESTIONS!

The sawfish is a very unusual ray. Ask a teacher or parent to help you learn about it. Figure out why this strange fish is a ray.

This is a sawfish. It looks very different from other rays, but they are still closely related.

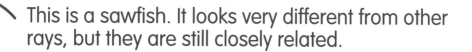

Think About It

A ray is a kind of fish. And fish have fins on their sides. Where are the fins on a ray?

One ray is called the bullseye electric ray. What do you think it looks like?

Some fish can change direction very quickly. Look at the ray's body. Do you think it can make quick turns?

Find Out More

BOOKS

Rustad, Martha E. H. *Stingrays*. Minneapolis: Bellwether Media, 2007.

WEB SITE

YouTube: Manta Rays Jumping
https://www.youtube.com/watch?v=-HkeGcj24K0
Watch this video of manta rays jumping out of the water in the Sea of Cortez.

Glossary

camouflage (KAM-uh-flahzh) to mask something so that it blends in with its surroundings

disk (DISK) an object that is round and flat

plankton (PLANK-tuhn) tiny floating plants and animals

prey (PRAY) animals that are eaten by other animals

saucer (SAW-sur) a small plate

shock (SHAHK) injury to the body caused by an electric current passing through it

snouts (SNOWTS) the front ends of animals' heads

Index

About the Author

Susan H. Gray is a zoologist. She has written many books about animals. She lives with her husband, Michael, in Cabot, Arkansas. They have many pets but do not own any rays.